Nashua Public Library

3 4517 011217412

DISCARDED

Nashua
Public
Library

Enjoy this book!
Please remember to return it on time
so that others may enjoy it too.

Manage your library account and
discover all we offer by visiting us
online at www.nashualibrary.org

Love your library? Tell a friend!

J

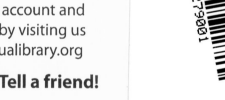

01279001

My First Pet
Snakes

by Vanessa Black

NASHUA PUBLIC LIBRARY

Bullfrog
Books

Ideas for Parents and Teachers

Bullfrog Books let children practice reading informational text at the earliest reading levels. Repetition, familiar words, and photo labels support early readers.

Before Reading

- Discuss the cover photo. What does it tell them?

- Look at the picture glossary together. Read and discuss the words.

Read the Book

- "Walk" through the book and look at the photos. Let the child ask questions. Point out the photo labels.

- Read the book to the child, or have him or her read independently.

After Reading

- Prompt the child to think more. Ask: What do you need to take care of a snake? Would you like one as a pet?

Bullfrog Books are published by Jump!
5357 Penn Avenue South
Minneapolis, MN 55419
www.jumplibrary.com

Copyright © 2017 Jump! International copyright reserved in all countries. No part of this book may be reproduced in any form without written permission from the publisher.

Library of Congress Cataloging-in-Publication Data

Names: Black, Vanessa, 1973- author.
Title: Snakes / by Vanessa Black.
Other titles: Bullfrog books. My first pet.
Description: Minneapolis, MN: Jump!, Inc., [2017]
Series: My first pet | Audience: Ages 5-8.
Audience: K to grade 3.
"Bullfrog Books are published by Jump!"
Includes bibliographical references and index.
Identifiers: LCCN 2016030069 (print)
LCCN 2016035424 (ebook)
ISBN 9781620315552 (hard cover: alk. paper)
ISBN 9781624965036 (e-book)
Subjects: LCSH: Snakes as pets—Juvenile literature.
Classification: LCC SF459.S5 B537 2017 (print)
LCC SF459.S5 (ebook) | DDC 639.3/96—dc23
LC record available at https://lccn.loc.gov/2016030069

Editor: Kirsten Chang
Book Designer: Molly Ballanger
Photo Researcher: Michelle Sonnek

Photo Credits: All photos by Shutterstock except: Alamy, 13, 22, 23bl; Fotolia, 5; Getty, 8–9, 20–21; Jonathan Crowe, 10–11, 23br; Thinkstock, 12, 18–19; 123RF, 17.

Printed in the United States of America at Corporate Graphics in North Mankato, Minnesota.

Table of Contents

A New Pet

May wants a snake.

There are many kinds.

5

May reads.

She learns about snakes.

What do snakes need?

Snakes need food.

Red eats a mouse.

Gulp! He eats it whole.

mouse

9

Snakes need water.

Hulk drinks.

He soaks in
the water, too.

Snakes need to shed.
Aidan puts out rocks.

12

skin

Jack rubs on them.

He sheds his skin.

Now he can grow bigger.

Snakes need to hide.

Rex has a cave.

He feels safe.

heat
lamp

Snakes need heat.

Lil has a heat lamp.

It keeps her warm.

Snakes need good care.
They can live a long time.
Hugs is 20 years old!

Snakes are cool pets!

What Does a Snake Need?

heat lamp or pad
Snakes are cold-blooded; most need a heat source to regulate their temperature.

glass tank
Snakes need tanks with locking tops so that they cannot escape.

hiding box
Most snakes like privacy when they eat. Make sure they have a place to hide.

shredded paper
Shredded paper makes good bedding. Use thick layers, and change it often.

water dish
Many snakes like to soak; make sure the water dish is big enough for the snake to crawl in.

Picture Glossary

heat
A high degree of warmth.

snake
A long, thin reptile without arms or legs.

shed
To lose old skin.

soaks
Lies in a liquid.

Index

To Learn More

Learning more is as easy as 1, 2, 3.

1) Go to www.factsurfer.com

2) Enter "petsnakes" into the search box.

3) Click the "Surf" button to see a list of websites.

With factsurfer.com, finding more information is just a click away.